THE SIMPLE TRUTHS
ABOUT DYING AND LIFE AFTER DEATH
IN THE WORLD OF SPIRIT AS TOLD
BY THE LATE LEILA CHEEK
TO HER HUSBAND

Allan Cheek

FANTINE PRESS

First published in 2006
by
E A Cheek
3 Seldon Avenue, Ryde
Isle of Wight PO33 1NR

in association with

FANTINE PRESS
The Coach House, Stansted Hall
Stansted, Essex CM24 8UD

British Library CIP Data:
A catalogue record of this book is
available from the British Library

ISBN 10: 1 901958 11 6
ISBN 13: 978 1 901958 11 9

Printed in England by Booksprint

ACKNOWLEDGEMENTS

My thanks to my son David and his wife Sue for their help in designing the cover and to Chris Boynton for the photograph on the cover.

Cover photograph: Chris Boynton, Island Photo Art
www.minigallery.co.uk/chrisboynton

CONTENTS

INTRODUCTION

COMMUNICATION

In 1963, I became interested in Spiritualism and, somewhat reluctantly, my wife joined me. Together we came to accept that there was life after death and that somewhere in a spirit realm dwelt our guardian angels, spirit guides and helpers, so every Thursday evening for over thirty years we have sat and prayed together and asked them to join us in sending our love to our family and friends and healing thoughts to those we knew to be in need of them.

In 1976, I had a near-death experience which confirmed my belief in a life after death.

In 1988, I read a book* which detailed several simple methods whereby one could contact the angels, so I tried one which was contact by writing. I was very pleased to find that it worked splendidly. I simply had to write a letter as though to a friend and then sit with my pen poised ready to write whatever came into my head. The answers I received were certainly not from my imagination.

Early on I learned the identity of the "go-between," one Wilhelm Tausner, a forester from Germany, married with two children. I asked him whether he had been in the army and he replied that he had been too young. He said his job now was to help people get together.

---

* *ASK YOUR ANGELS*
  by Alma Daniel, Timothy Wyllie and Andrew Romer
  Published by Piatkus Ltd.

I asked him "Do you like where you are now?" and he replied: "Yes, very much. It makes me very happy to help others in this way." Apparently, he is able to read and transmit my thoughts and then receive and dictate the replies to me telepathically. I have been writing these letters now for over seven years and in that time have come to regard Wilhelm and the other guides and helpers as close personal friends which is why I now start my letters "Dear Angels and Special Friends."

The Angels prefer to remain anonymous. When I asked whether they were involved in the replies I received, I was told, "The words we give you often come from them in the first place. They guide us to guide you. They know what goes on," but when I asked whether I could be given the name of one of them I was told "It doesn't matter what name I have so long as you know I am here."

Over the years, my *Special Friends* have given me guidance as to the manner of our relationship:- "Think of us as your constant companions." "We are conversing with you even when you don't know it." "Think of what your life would be like if you had no friends to turn to - your instincts would lead you on. We are your instincts." "Keep talking to us and you will find that what we are saying is true and that will make your faith firmer." "We are very happy to be in touch with someone who acknowledges us and is in regular contact with us. We are here to help all we can." "We enjoy these 'chats.' It certainly is a different life-line from the usual clairvoyance and much more personal contact." "For you this is proof that there really is life after death - we are very much alive." "We all enjoy chatting with you and knowing that you are aware of us and our presence with you." "Pray for us. We hear your prayers and are grateful for them because they come with your love." "We are always busy looking after you and planning for you and are happy doing it. We never leave you." "We know what you are thinking - we know you very well." "Your knowledge of us and regular contacts makes it so much easier for us."

My written letters and their replies soon developed into question and answer sessions, rather like instant e-mails. I asked them many questions about their life in their world and received many fascinating answers but I will return to them later...

Allan and Leila Cheek on their wedding day, 9th May 1945

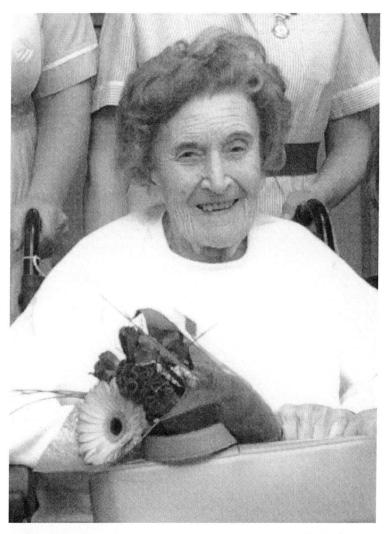

Leila Cheek, aged 91, the first patient in the new ward of the Earl Mountbatten Hospice in the Isle of Wight on April 30th 2005. She died three days later just six days before her sixtieth wedding anniversary.

CHAPTER ONE

THE RECOVERY

On May 3rd, 2005, my darling wife Leila died in the Earl Mountbatten Hospice in the Isle of Wight: she was aged 91. The death certificate showed 'ovarian cancer' as the cause of death. She died six days short of our sixtieth wedding anniversary.

Two days later I wrote to my "Angels and Special Friends."

May 5th
Me:- Please take special care of Leila for me.
Them:- Don't worry: she is in very good hands. She has had a trying time and it will take a while for her to recover.
Me:- Please give her my love.
Them:- We will.

May 11th
Them:- Leila has met her Dad - it made her very happy. She is still recovering from her ordeal of the past two years and especially the last few weeks. We are taking care of her. She is much more rested and is beginning to adjust to her new way of life.

May 14th
Them:- Leila is well. She is still recovering but is doing well. Knowing that you are in touch in this way is a great comfort to her and is a great help.

May 15th

Me:- Today was Leila's funeral. Was she there?

Them:- Yes, with our help.

Me:- I hope she was not too sad.

Them:- Not at all. You made it quite clear that it was not an occasion for mourning or grief but gratitude and thanksgiving and she was pleased with that.

May 20th

Me:- Today David (our son) planted Leila's ashes on Brading Down. Was Leila there? If so, how did she feel?

Them:- Yes, she was there She had happy memories of Brading Down and was pleased by the thought. As for her feelings, she felt only love for David and Sue.

Me:- How is Leila now? Is she still recovering?

Them:- Yes, she is gradually getting better all the time.

Me:- Has she met any of her old friends?

Them:- Yes, lots of them - Joyce, Nora and many more.

Me:- That should have made her and them very happy.

Them:- It did. Such reunions are always a pleasure here and strengthen the true reality of a new life here.

Me:- My Mum and Dad must have been pleased to see her again.

Them:- Yes, they were very fond of her and she of them.

May 23rd

Them:- Leila is well and happy and sends her love. She says, "Don't worry about me." She is being well looked after.

May 25th

Me:- How is Leila now please? Is there anything I can do to help?

Them:- Yes, carry on keeping in touch as often as you can until she gets really settled. Knowing you are still in touch in this way has given her the best possible start.

May 31st

Me:- I planted the trough in the porch today - not as well as Leila but I tried.

Them:- She was watching you do it and was very pleased with the result.

Me:- Here I am chatting away instead of going to bed just as Leila and I so often did.

Them:- She remembers it well and laughs.

June 1st

Me:- Is there anything that is bothering her that she would like me to do? How about the silver?

Them:- She says "Yes please." She would be very happy if you did that.

Me:- Anything else?

Them:- No, but she enjoys thinking about it because it reinforces the reality of being in touch.

Me:- I'm glad. Is she happy now?

Them:- Yes, very. She has met many people - friends, relatives and family she was so happy to see again.

June 3rd

Me:- Please tell Leila I have done the silver. I hope she approved.

Them:- She certainly did and thanks you very much. "You did a splendid job," she says. She was especially pleased to see her father's photo frame and salver shine again.

Me:- I'm glad. How is she? Has she fully recovered yet?

Them:- Yes, completely, and is very happy here. She says it is a great relief to have no pain or discomfort and please give David and Sue her love for all their kindness to you.

CHAPTER TWO

A NEW WAY OF LIFE

June 7th
Me:- Can Leila tell me yet anything about her new way of life over there? Where does she live? Does she live alone or share with other people? And how about clothes - are they the same as here? And so on. I am very interested.
Them:- Yes - we can see that. She lives in a nice house. The lovely life she led means that unknowingly she has furnished it herself to her own taste and very nicely too. She is very happy in it - it is her own place. She dresses as she always did - she can choose whatever she likes in her own mind, perhaps a little younger than recently. As for getting out and about she has only to think of someone and they automatically arrive or she will find herself with them. These are no difficulties here. Everything is quiet, serene and happy.

June 11th
Me:- Is Leila there now please?
Them:- Yes, she is and sends her love. She watched you reading your letters to her from India tonight. They brought back many memories for her and made her very happy.

June 13th
Me:- I was thinking of Leila as I sat drinking hot Horlicks and how we sat together in the night when we couldn't sleep, just sipping our drinks in a companionable silence.
Them:- Yes, she saw you and knew what you were thinking

She knows you were thinking of her with love and she was thinking the same as you.

Me:- It's nice to know we can still share these moments together.

Them:- Yes, she treasures the contact between you.

Me:- I have just packed Leila's sewing things. She was an expert needlewoman. Will she be able to do that where she is now?

Them:- Yes, but only for pleasure. There is no need to make clothes. Leila thanks you for coming to write. She looks forward to these chats like she used to look forward to your letters from India.

June 14th

Me:- I received the video tape of Leila being interviewed in the new ward of the hospice today. Did Leila watch it too?

Them:- Yes, she was with you and David and was glad you liked it.

June 15th 3.25 a.m.

Me:- I'm sure I heard Leila say she had something to tell me.

Them:- Yes. She wanted to tell you about her latest adventure - she is really excited about it. She has been to a meeting. Many of the people she knew from her past were there and she was the guest of honour. There were speeches extolling her many virtues - all very flattering and she was quite overcome. She says she knew you would be pleased for her.

Me:- Of course I am. I wonder who organised the meeting?

Them:- Her angels. It never occurred to her that she had her own angels looking after her. They could do nothing to prevent the pain but helped her to bear it which she did splendidly.

Me:- Please give my thanks to her angels.

Them:- We will.

Me:- When you say "we," to whom do you refer please?

Them:- Your angels and us, your guides.

Me:- Is there anybody among the guides I don't know?

Them:- Yes, several. You have a whole team of people looking after you all the time.

Me:- Whoever you are I send you my most grateful thanks. Please tell Leila I am not only delighted about the meeting but also because she felt she was able to get in touch with me so easily to tell me about it.

Them:- She was so excited and overcome she wanted to tell you about it right away.

Me:- I'm glad she did.

June 17th

Me:- Now that the initial excitement will be dying down, I imagine Leila will be up and doing again.

Them:- She will be shown what activities are available and left to make her own choice when she is ready. There is so much.

June 20th

Me:- Elaine and Paul were married on Saturday. Was Leila there too?

Them:- Yes, she was. She, too, enjoyed the very happy occasion and she thought the wedding dress was lovely.

Me:- I'm reading poetry at Newport on Tuesday. I hope Leila will be there and likes what I have written.

Them:- She says she has already read it and although some of it made her sad, she is proud of you for having written it. Yes, she will be there.

June 21st

Them:- She is still recovering well from all the suffering she has had over several years and it takes a time to fade out of one's system.

June 22nd.

Me:- Were you there at the poetry reading?

Them:- Yes, we were there and so was Leila, very close to you and David. She says go again and keep up the contact.

June 23rd

Me:- Have you done anything exciting today?

Leila:- No. I have spent most of the time thinking about us and our memories. I was very touched by your poetry reading last night.

Me:- David hopes to join me in the Thursday prayers this evening. I hope you will be there too.

Leila:- Of course I will. I realise now how much love it generates over here - much more than we ever thought.

June 24th

Them:- Leila has been meeting up with friends and relatives - they have so much to talk about! She is doing very well and these contacts help enormously.

June 25th

Leila:- Although you can't see or feel me, I am still very close to you. There is so much to learn about this new way of life and I have a lot of learning to do so I'll be very near you for a long time yet.

Me:- I'm so pleased for you that you are free from pain and discomfort at last.

Leila:- So am I, even though it means we have to be apart physically for a while. Please give my love to the family. I miss being with them physically too, although I am closer to them all more often. It is wonderful to know how very real their love for us has been.

July 1st

Me:- I have just been listening to Leila's memoirs on tape again.

Leila:- Yes, I heard them too. They brought back many happy memories for me.

Me:- In your last tape, you mentioned our belief that those who have 'gone ahead' watch over those still here. Have you been able to 'watch over' anybody yet?

Leila:- Oh, yes, all the time. It is marvellous to be able to flit from one person to another in an instant and to know what they are thinking about and what their innermost worries are, but I have yet to learn how I can best help them.

July 7th

Leila:- I have been busy today. There is so much to learn here. It is like being back at school again but wonderful, quite incredible in fact.

Me:- I'm glad you are enjoying it.

Leila:- Oh, I am!

Me:- Have you had any surprising encounters with old friends yet?

Leila:- Yes, several I had quite forgotten but was glad to be reminded of.

July 9th

Me:- Thinking of the fun we have shared. I loved the sound of your laughter. I wish I had recorded it.

Leila:- I know, but be glad for me that I am free from pain at last and able to enjoy life all over again.

Me:- Have you been doing anything new lately?

Leila:- Yes, all the time. Everything is new to me. I'm like a schoolgirl in her first term but everybody is so kind and helpful.

Me:- Who is "everybody"?

Leila:- Our guides and helpers - people who have been caring for us for years and know us intimately. I only imagined them before but now I find that they are very real. They are so glad you know them so well and thank them as you do.

July 15th
Me:- Thank you for being with me last evening at the poetry reading. I was very much aware of your presence and grateful for your support.
Them:- Yes, we were all there and enjoyed the evening. You did well again. Well done!
Me:- Thank you. How is Leila now please?
Them: She is fine - very well and very happy, quite excited about all the new things she has learned to do. She is a very good pupil.
Me:- Did she see the golf on TV?
Them:- Yes, she did. She was watching it with you sitting in her usual chair and glad she didn't feel the heat as much as you did.
Me:- Thank you for that. Please give her my love.
Them:- She knows you love her and sends you her love.

July 16th
Me:- I thought you were watching the golf on TV, with me but Jeremy (our second son) thought you were watching it with him.
Leila:- You were both right. I started with Jeremy but then switched over to be with you. My thanks and love to both of you for thinking of me.
Me:- What new things have you been learning lately?
Leila:- All sorts of things - how to help people by inserting your thoughts into their minds and how to communicate without knowing other languages.
Me:- It all sounds wonderful to me.
Leila:- It is, and I'm thoroughly enjoying it.

Me:- Who is teaching you?
Leila:- My angels and guides, who are lovely.

July 17th
Me:- I received a photograph of you all nicely framed from the photographer. I thought it was beautiful.
Leila:- Yes, I liked it too. I'm better looking in it than I can remember. In fact, I hardly recognise it as me. Anyway, thank you for loving me so much. It makes such a difference to me here to feel your love for me, and the love of the boys and their families I feel much more acutely here and am very grateful to them. Please give all of them my love.

July 26th
Me:- Helen phoned me this evening and asked me to send her love to Leila.
Them:- Leila heard your phone call from Helen so already knew her message.
Me:- Is Leila here tonight?
Them: No, she is resting. She has had a busy time lately.

July 27th
Me:- How are you now? You were resting yesterday.
Leila:- I am better now I have had a rest.
Me:- Do you rest on a bed?
Leila:- Yes, of course, although it's a bit lonely without you by my side.

July 28th
Them:- Leila is very well and very happy. She has been busy learning more about her new life - so similar to yours in some ways but so different in many others.
Me:- Any instructions, please?
Them:- No. Just carry on as you are and keep writing. Leila treasures this contact with you and sends her love.

July 30th

Me:- I have been with my cousin Judy this afternoon. She was very low in spirits. Did Leila put the idea in my head to go and see Judy?

Them:- Yes. She knew Judy would appreciate a visit from you and needed cheering up.

Me:- I'm glad she did and also interested in this new development that she can transmit her ideas to me in this way.

July 31st

Me:- David and I enjoyed the air show. I hope you did too.

Leila:- Yes, thank you. I enjoyed being with you both when you were both so happy together.

August 2nd

Me:- Three months into your new life! Has it seemed very long?

Leila:- No, it certainly hasn't. In fact, it seems almost no time at all. I was recovering at first but since then I've been so busy it seems no time at all.

Me:- David's son Jo came down for the day yesterday and we had lunch with David. He is well and happy.

Leila:- Yes, I know. I was with you all the time. Don't worry about your operation tomorrow. I know it is a nuisance but it will turn out all right in the end.

Me:- Thank you. You seem to be in the prediction business now. Are there any things I can be looking forward to now?

Leila:- Yes, but I'm not allowed to tell you at this stage so you will just have to be patient.

Me:- Have you seen an angel? What does an angel look like?

Leila:- Yes, I have. They are lovely,. They can change their appearance and those I met were very charming people.

24

August 8th

Me:- Were you with David at our prayer meeting tonight?
Leila: Yes, I was. It was fascinating seeing so many people there too - mostly the people we have always prayed for but many more come just for the experience.

August 10th

Them:- Leila was watching you as you went through your photograph albums and recalled many happy memories.

August 14th

Leila:- I am very well and happy. Everyone is so kind and patient. I'm learning all the time.
Me:- Have you had a chance to spend more time with your Dad?
Leila:- Yes, and it was lovely to be so close to him again and we could laugh together again.

August 21st

Them:- Leila says someone has bought her handkerchiefs from the hospice shop and she was pleased with that.

August 27th

Me:- I watched the video and listened to the tapes of your memoirs this evening.
Leila:- I, too, watched the video and listened to the tapes. It is strange listening to your own voice.

August 29th

Leila:- I'm learning so much more. So much of it is quite new to me but increasingly wonderful and everyone is so kind and helpful.

August 31st

Me:- What colour is Leila's hair now? She kept it brown by

using a colour rinse. I don't know if she can do that now.
Them:- Yes, she does, and she can make it any other colour she likes but it is always brown just as it has always been for years and it suits her very well.

September 3rd
Leila:- I am having a very happy time here. Life here is wonderful.

September 9th
Them:- Leila says thank you for the birthday wishes. She misses the cards but has a new birthday now.

September 12th
Me:- Jeremy is asking whether Leila is able to foresee future events?
Leila:- Yes, in a limited way and like all of us not allowed to divulge such knowledge as we have. There are many things we have to learn here that probably seem difficult for you to understand but they are all part of a pattern of higher learning which you will come to share with us one day.

September 15th
Me:- I was watching the video of Leila's TV interview this evening.
Them:- Yes, we were watching it too, just before we joined you in your prayer meeting. Thank you for your prayers - they mean a lot to us.
Me:- I was watching the golf earlier. Was Leila watching that too?
Them: Yes, she was there with you remembering how you watched it together too.

September 18th
Leila:- We have so much to be grateful for. Let us be happy

even though we are separated in this way. The past is gone but our love remains.

September 18th
Me:- It is wonderful to know that you can still be so close to me.

Leila:- I certainly am much more than you know! I can do this because we are both so much in love it makes a bond between us. I wish you could feel me kiss you.

September 21st
Them:- We were there with you at the poetry reading. Leila appreciated the poem about how brave she was when it came to saying "Goodbye," and recalled the various partings.

Me:- Any news or instructions please?

Them:- Yes, do something about your hair.

September 22nd
Them:- Well done! Your hair looks better.

Me:- Leila said that she and Madeleine "got on famously" and that Madeleine had been very helpful.

Them:- Yes, they had a common bond - they both loved you.

Me:- I'm glad there appears to be no room for jealousy in your world.

Them:- Certainly not. We are only concerned with positive thoughts.

September 27th
Me:- I put the photo of you in the hospice in a frame earlier. I hope you like it.

Leila:- Yes, I do but I prefer the photo in the album you were looking at earlier. I really was good looking then, wasn't I?

Me:- I'll say so. You were gorgeous.

Leila:- Nice of you to say so.

September 30th
Them:- Leila says yes, she is in bed with you when you get there, so go to bed now.

October 4th
Me:- I bought a new pot plant for the lounge today. I hope you like it.
Leila:- Yes, I do. I think it looks very nice.
Me:- Do you have any flowers where you are?
Leila:- Yes, and they are beautiful.
Me:- What are you learning now?
Leila:- The way the system works here and how it all fits in. It certainly is a vast organisation.

October 6th
Me:- I felt very close to you this evening.
Leila:- Yes, I was there and very close to you.
Me:- I thought you kissed me.
Leila:- I did, on your right cheek.
Me:- Have you had a happy day?
Leila:- Yes, very happy. All the people here are so lovely and kind and loving all the time. Every day is a joy.

October 11th
Me:- How are you?
Leila:- I'm fine and really enjoying life. Everything is so beautiful and quiet and lovely, and all the people I have met have been wonderfully kind and helpful and generally loving. This is very much like being in school again but far more enjoyable. You will love it here.

October 16th
Me:- How do you look back on all our years together?
Leila:- Wonderful. Together we built a special relationship through sixty years which has now produced a solid base

for giving us both a wonderful start in this life. I'm fine and very happy. We are so lucky - we have such wonderful friends here who are all very kind to me.

October 18th

Me:- Do you remember dying, and if so, what was it like?

Leila:- It was wonderful - all very peaceful and restful after the pain and discomfort I had been having. At first, I just relaxed and rested then someone I took to be a nurse asked me to get up and then together we simply walked out of the room into another in another place. She gave me a bed and made me comfortable, told me to go to sleep and left. The room was large, sunlit and beautiful and I was the only one in it. There were flowers everywhere. I was very tired and glad of a proper sleep.

I don't know how long I slept but when I woke up, my dad was there so I knew right away what had happened. I was so happy to see him I cried. We chatted happily for a while then he got up to go, telling me to go to sleep again, which I did. That happened several times. Each time I woke up, I had new visitors - Joyce and Nora were first so I had no time to feel unhappy. Then the 'nurse' lady told me you had been in touch asking after me and sending your love and I was overjoyed to learn you had been in touch so quickly and easily and I still am.

Later a group of several people I didn't know came in and greeted me very affectionately, saying they were and had been our guides and helpers and were there to nurse me back to health and to take care of me, and they were all so lovely and kind. They also promised me that when I was well again I would be able to get in touch with you direct. I was thrilled to hear that and couldn't wait. I think the rest you know.

October 20th

Leila:- I have been asked to join a group of ladies coping with introducing children of all ages to their new surroundings and getting them 'acclimatised' to the point where they can successfully move on to somewhere more appropriate to their needs. I understand there are many such groups as ours being set up.

October 21st

Me:- Are the children a mixture of nationalities, and are they sorted into age groups? I'm sure they will have a wonderfully happy time with you.

Leila:- Yes, they do. There is a lot of laughter. My group is aged 8-10 and come from everywhere.

Me:- Are they upset leaving their parents?

Leila:- At first they are but they quickly get over it. They are probably still sad when they have a quiet moment to themselves but seem happy to join my group.

Me:- How many are there?

Leila:- About forty.

Leila:- Our Thursday prayers were more popular than ever this week. All our old friends were there and the family of course, but our prayers seem to have set going a wider realisation of life in this world which more people who have been here for a long time hadn't realised.

October 22nd

Me:- Have you learned anything lately?

Leila:- Yes, but they are difficult to explain. So much of it is thought. The incredible thing is it is all so marvellous and yet it is all so simple. On earth we never get around to using our thoughts in this way. And there is so much of it! We never get tired of learning more because it is all so enjoyable and, of course, our guides and helpers who have been here so much longer than we have are a wonderful help.

Me:- Jeremy had his knee operation today.

Leila:- Yes, they knew all about it and were there with him.

Me:- I'm looking at the photo of our family reunion a year ago. Little did we realise it would be our last.

Leila:- I know, I'm looking at it too. Never mind; it's just one of thousands of happy memories we share.

October 24th

Leila:- I come to be with you as often as I can when I'm not busy with my lessons and the children. They are lovely and remind me of the time when I was a Sunday School teacher.

Me:- I remember reading years ago that people in your world can choose what age they want to be but usually gravitate backwards or forwards to middle age. Have you changed at all?

Leila:- Yes, I have changed. Now I feel so fit and well and happy. I feel better in younger clothes and feel younger, straighter and taller.

Me:- Is your hair the same colour?

Leila:- Not quite. I have it a bit lighter now.

October 25th

Them:- Leila is doing very well and is very happy and we are happy to see her so happy. Your contact and support have given her the best possible start. She has made such good progress that she might soon be able to move on to the next learning stage - like going up a class in school.

October 27th

Me:- I had an Alexander Technique lesson from Sue this afternoon. Were you there and was anyone else there?

Leila:- Yes, I was there all the time and found it very interesting 'hearing' what Sue was thinking. Yes, there were others there too - all our guides and helpers interested in your welfare.

Me:- It must have been crowded in that little room!

Leila:- Space has no meaning for us.

Me:- Jeremy phoned and said he was doing well after his operation. I said I was sure you had a hand in his healing.

Leila:- Yes, we did, and that was interesting too. You have no idea how many people were involved!

November 5th
Them:- Leila is doing a splendid job with the children but took the time to look in on you and Jeremy and was pleased you were having such a happy time together.

November 10th
Me:- Any news of Leila, please?

Them:- Yes, she is very happy and has been with you all the evening.

November 15th
Me:- I hope you liked the poetry reading this evening.

Leila:- Yes, I did. I liked the first poem best because it brought back the happiest memory. I'm glad you have ordered the oil and also had tea with the Phillips - I'm sure they appreciated you calling in.

Summary

In the first six months since Leila's death I had learned the following:-

1. She had "wonderful" memories of actually dying.
2. She was not sad at the funeral.
3. She was happy when her ashes were laid on Brading Down.
4. She was helped to recover from her painful ordeal.
5. Her father and friends had been alerted to her arrival and organised into a series of visits while she recovered.
6. Guides and helpers came to nurse her back to health.
7. She had frequent helpful contacts with her guides and helpers, and met angels, who were "charming."
8. She found herself in her own house furnished to her taste. Within it is a bed on which she can rest. Outside there are beautiful flowers.
9. She found she had only to think of someone and either
   (a) they instantly appeared with her, or
   (b) she instantly appeared with them.
10. She can 'flit' at will to be in constant touch with members of the family and visiting old friends.
11. She can read what is in people's minds and know their innermost worries.
12. She can insert her thoughts into their minds.
13. She can converse with others in any language.
14. She can revisit her old home, watch TV and sit in her old chair.
15. She can watch our activities and hear our conversations. She can hear both sides of a telephone conversation, can read what I have written and hear tape recordings and watch video.
16. She and our guides and helpers have accompanied me at various social events such as the Thursday prayer meetings and poetry readings.

17. She is having daily lessons explaining the new world in which she is living.

18. She has been busy helping a group of about forty children from various countries aged 8-10, acclimatising them to their new life before moving on.

19. She feels she is younger, taller and straighter.

20. She wears younger clothes. Her hair is a shade lighter.

According to our 'Special friends,' my frequent written contacts gave Leila "the best possible start." When I wrote to Leila regarding her direct contact with me she replied, "I can do this because we are both so much in love it makes a bond between us."

CHAPTER THREE

INFORMATION FROM THE GUIDES

So far I have quoted extracts from the 267 pages of 'letters' I have written since Leila's death, omitting the many intimate exchanges reminiscent of the love letters we wrote to each other when I was serving in the army in India during the war but as I mentioned in the Introduction, I have been writing these 'letters' for over seven years. In that time, I have written over 500 pages and received many fascinating replies to my enquiries regarding life in the spirit world. Having deleted the many repetitions, particularly those telling me how much my guides enjoyed our 'chats,' I have sorted the remainder into a number of headings as follows:-

God - The Creator - The Lord

Me:- Can you explain about God to me? I can think of a Creator who brought life to and controls all forms of life on earth but to think of the universe is way beyond me.

Them:- Yes, there is an all-powerful Creator in charge of the spirit realm surrounding the earth whom we call God. On the other hand, we do not question as to what limits there are, if any, to his powers regarding the rest of the universe.

Them:- We went to a big rally recently which we all enjoyed. We were summoned to attend and we all met up in a big arena. There was a beautiful choir and we all received a special blessing from the Lord. We left feeling very happy and very blessed.

Organisation - Progress

Me:- Your world must involve a vast organisation. Can you tell me more?

Them:- It would take too long to give you the details but what it amounts to is that we are here in the first class at the bottom level, and later there is the possibility of progress through an enormous number of channels to an endless range of higher levels. The channel through which you progress will be the one most appropriate for you so you will always be happy in whatever you are doing.

Religions

Me:- All the religions go on about a judgement and a re-run of one's life. Have you seen any evidence of that?

Them:- It may exist but we haven't seen it.

Life in the Spirit World

Them:- We are very happy here. We do as we wish but find the most rewarding thing is to help others in any way we can. Then we have to learn the different ways in which we can influence people and events. And then our greatest joy is to know that those we have known and loved still remember and love us and come to know we love them still. And there are times when we need to be forgiven so that love can begin anew.

Me:- Where do you live? Do you live in houses?

Them:- We certainly do and very nice they are too. You will feel at home instantly over here.

Me:- Do you have a social life or is it all communal activities?

Them:- Oh no, we can join in anything we like or work on our own if we choose. Attendance is not regular or compulsory like going to work on earth.

Me:- And without physical bodies. I suppose you never get hungry and never eat!

36

Them:- We go through the motions of eating just the same but we don't have to think of our figures so we can eat what we like. You will enjoy it, I'm sure.

Me:- Do you people ever sleep at all?

Them:- No. We really only sleep when we first arrive but soon realise that it is a bodily habit so is unnecessary here, but we can rest if we feel tired. We are always conscious of how wonderful all this is and how lucky we are to be here.

Them:- Your mother paints, your father has his garden, your brother Bertie is busy learning. Bertie has just finished a job that was also a milestone in his spiritual development.

Them:- This world is full of love. Nobody wants for anything.

Christmas

Them:- We always get together for Christmas. It is a joyful time for us because much love is freely given. The love you spread to others is a great blessing to all. It is important, and you are greatly blessed in return. And you always have our love too.

Time

(to M. who died in 1947)

Me:- Does it seem a long time to you?

M.:- No. Time does not matter here. Only the happiness arising from our work remains in our memories.

Spirit Guides

Me:- Does each one of my guides have any special ability or do they all work together?

Them:- Both. It all depends on how they can best help at the time.

Me:- How did they come to pick on me? Were they chosen

or did they volunteer? After all, none of them knew me.

Them:- They have a temporary attachment before deciding to take on a full time job.

Me:- Do one's guides stay the same or do they change?

Them:- Yes, they change as your circumstances change, but yours haven't changed for a long time so neither have we.

Me:- Are Sophocles, Red Cloud and Brother Paul still my guides? Years ago, before I knew who they were, they were very much involved in writing my book *QUEST*, a search for believable beliefs, which is still selling and has been referred to as a 'spiritual classic.'

Them:- Yes, they are still with you in a sort of supervisory capacity watching over your spiritual development.

EARTH CONNECTIONS

Birth

Me:- How does a soul get involved with a baby?

Them:- It takes a conscious decision to start life again knowing that it will face oblivion for a while in a new life, then focuses on the growing cells.

Me:- B. lost her baby today. What, if anything, would happen to that baby in your world or was it too young to qualify?

Them:- A soul selected to be born in that child. When the baby fails to mature for medical reasons, the spirit is free to return whence it came, free to make another attempt to enter the human world if it so desires, which may be with the original parents if they are intent on having another child.

Death

Me:- Meta is in a poor way today. How long will it last?

Them:- We can't say. That is for a higher decision.

Me:- How is Meta getting on in her new life?

Them:- Don't worry – we are taking care of her. Things are a bit strange for her here yet. She saw you kiss her head in the nursing home before she finally passed over and wanted to thank you.

Them:- Come to realise that life on earth is like a small introductory phase, basic learning like that of a young child, so don't be alarmed at the thought of your first term ending. There is so much to look forward to.
Me:- And when might that be?
Them:- That is not under our control.

Me:- Why didn't B.'s husband (ex-RAF) get in touch? *Them:-* The manner of his death was so traumatic that it took him a long time to adjust to a whole new situation he didn't know existed and knew nothing about the possibility of communication, so he resigned himself to carrying on with his new life alone, but your contact today has opened up a whole new concept and channel of communication for him for which he is very grateful. Now that he can be in touch with her again, he will be with her very much more and she will feel his presence with her all the time.

Pattern
Them:- Wisdom is in knowing when not to ask but to accept that the pattern is ordained.

Them:- We are interested in your memoirs. You will see the pattern in your life more clearly as you write.

Planning
Them:- Wait a while and you will see that we have been busy on your behalf.
Me:- Thank you. You must enjoy having secrets.
Them:- We do, especially when we know our efforts are appreciated.

Me:- Can you tell me what it is?
Them:- No. It is still being worked out.

Them:- We think you will be pleased with what we have in store for you. We have been working on it for some time.

Me:- (Re. Meta) Looking after her affairs was a chore but I was glad to help. It was probably meant to be and I have to accept things as they are.
Them:- Yes, it was all planned that way. You have done well.

Them:- We have been working on your behalf. These things take time and never happen quickly, but be patient and we hope you will be pleased when you see what we have been up to. We have a different idea of time. Place your trust in us and we will work it out for you.

Me:- I have met a lady and through her met a man involved in screen writing who kindly gave me the names of the best people to whom I should submit the film script I have written.
Them:- Yes, we knew you were going to meet up and get in touch with each other in this way - the culmination of a very long process involving a great many people.

Me:- I'm sure you will lead me into something else soon.
Them:- Yes, we are working on it so don't be surprised at whatever turns up.

Prediction
Me:- Have you any news for me about what lies ahead?
Them:- Yes. Meta's affairs will soon be sorted out satisfactorily. David's house purchase will go through and the New Year will be a very happy one for him.

Them:- Don't worry about the hospital trip. We will be there for you.

Them:- You will be involved in something else new soon that will give you much pleasure (we enjoy having secrets) while you can enjoy looking forward to it.

Them:- You will be having a very happy time this week with your family.

Them:- David will get some good news soon and Jeremy's trip will be successful. You will be doing something new again soon (exciting, isn't it?).
Me:- Thank you for watching over all the family. Come to think of it, you are well and truly busy with all that lot!
Them:- Yes, we are but we enjoy doing it and your knowing about it makes us even happier.

Them:- Now that Meta's affairs are finished we have good news of things in store for you - a wonderful time blessed by your own angels and all of us in the spirit world. Don't worry about anything - it will all happily unfold under our guidance. Your health will go on improving.

Involvement
Me:- I expect you had a hand in getting Meta's affairs settled and in David's decision to buy a house here.
Them:- Yes, we did.

Me:- Jeremy flies to Egypt today. Will you and Leila be going to look after him?
Them:- Of course. That is easy for us.

Me:- Thank you for giving me the words of the poetry.
Them:- You are most welcome (that's from all of us).

Them:- Your Dad says he wishes hearing aids like yours had been available in his day.

Me:- Tell him he was very brave and patient and bore his deafness well.

Them:- He says "Thank you."

Through these 'letters,' my brother Bertie has enjoyed recalling the days when we went cycling together and rode his motorcycle together and played hockey together and so on.

Me:- Having only recently come to fully appreciate your total involvement in all my activities, I feel I should apologise for not having acknowledged it sooner, so my apologies to one and all.

Them:- That wasn't necessary but appreciated all the same.

Healing

Me:- Can you tell me more about healing please?

Them:- Yes, we gather in a group and pray for whoever needs healing. It doesn't take long but we can feel it is being effective. One of the guides or helpers is sent to attend the patient and supervise and report progress. We meet regularly to maintain contact.

Me:- Can you tell me, please, whether there is anything I can do to help heal myself?

Them:- Try to recognise that this is a time of trial for you spiritually, not just physically. By recognising our presence and invoking our help you are already healing yourself.

Me:- Is there anything else I can do?

Them:- Yes. Get rid of the negative thoughts about all that has been happening. Look ahead to a bright future and be glad of all the pleasure you have given others.

Flowers

Them:- Flowers are close to us and we are close to the flowers. You have only to smell a flower to be nearer to God for a moment.

Them:- Even mundane things have a spiritual element and significance eventually.

EPILOGUE

Me:- I am surprised at the way people I have spoken to so readily accept the reality of your world, our letter-writing contacts and Leila's new way of life. No one has been as sceptical as we might have expected.
Them:- You are playing a small part in a vast movement that is really only just beginning, but every contact you make is important. We are here to support you in this work.

CONCLUSION - THE SIMPLE TRUTHS

Don't expect anything 'spooky' when you die. You will be exactly the same one minute after death as you were before, except that any pain or discomfort will disappear. If you have been ill, you will be lovingly nursed back to health.

A group of people will come to meet you - ordinary people such as you would meet wherever you are now, dressed and speaking just as you would expect them to. They will inform you that they are your guides and helpers and have known you intimately for a long time. They love you and are there to look after you. When you are well enough, they will teach you all about your new way of life. For you these lessons will be like starting in school again only much more enjoyable.

You will have many happy reunions with your family and friends, all the people you have known and loved, and you will quickly realise that they still love you. If you wish, you will be shown how to make contact with those you have left behind but remember that this has to be a two-way contact and will not be possible if they refuse to accept that such communication is possible. You will, however, soon learn how you can have fun flitting around following their activities. You will also be able to join in healing prayers on their behalf.

In the meantime, you can welcome your own angels and *Special Friends*. They are already there with you and have been closely involved with you for a long time, but they will greatly appreciate your acknowledgement of their presence. They tell me that this makes the work they are doing on one's behalf very much easier. You, too, will come to accept that these are real people, not just figments of your imagination.

The world of spirit is a reality and the people in it are real. My wife Leila is there among them and is very happy and all the people she has met are very happy too.

So there you have it - one continuing life here and in the world of spirit, the continuing love of those we have known and loved, and the loving presence of others we do not know. These are the simple truths. But I cannot finish this book without mentioning my great personal indebtedness to my angels and *Special Friends*. I have learned of their total involvement in my personal life over many very difficult years and their love and support have been a major factor in my total recovery from a series of serious illnesses plus giving me the strength to cope with my wife's long battle with cancer at the same time. I am hoping that this little book will be instrumental in leading many others to share that same love and support which is so readily available by simply accepting the presence of their own *Special Friends* as a real and continuing factor in their daily lives.